CW00672532

# NINE LESSONS FROM THE DARK

# NINE LESSONS
# FROM THE DARK

Adam Thorpe

CAPE POETRY

Published by Jonathan Cape 2003

2 4 6 8 10 9 7 5 3 1

First published in Great Britain in 2003 by
Jonathan Cape
Random House, 20 Vauxhall Bridge Road, London SW1V 2SA

Random House Australia (Pty) Limited
20 Alfred Street, Milsons Point, Sydney,
New South Wales 2061, Australia

Random House New Zealand Limited
18 Poland Road, Glenfield,
Auckland 10, New Zealand

Random House South Africa (Pty) Limited
Endulini, 5A Jubilee Road, Parktown 2193, South Africa

The Random House Group Limited Reg. No. 954009
www.randomhouse.co.uk

A CIP catalogue record for this book is available from the British Library

ISBN 0-224-06385-5

Papers used by Random House are natural,
recyclable products made from wood grown in sustainable forests;
the manufacturing processes conform to the environmental
regulations of the country of origin

Typeset by Palimpsest Book Production Limited
Polmont, Stirlingshire

Printed and bound in Great Britain by
Biddles Ltd, Guildford and King's Lynn

*When a cloud is not on the mind the sky clouds*

Ivor Gurney

# CONTENTS

# ACKNOWLEDGEMENTS

With grateful thanks to the following publications where some of these poems first appeared: *Hudson Review, The Times Literary Supplement, Metre, London Review of Books, PN Review.*

'Honesty' was commissioned for broadcast by BBC Radio 3's *The Verb.*

# CAIRN

Like a person, spookish, spying from on high
over the whispering of marram on the brae,

it stretched up out of a slew of scree
to be this: the peak's thank-offering to the sky,

our hike's lynchpin. And the sky was clear
when we started out, singing even up the sheerest

parts, enthusiasm roped to our
excellent spirits. Then the clouds thickened and the four

showers blurred into one − the going far more slur
than stone. Boots squeaked like tholes against the oar

and we lost the cairn, vanished somewhere in layer
upon layer of grey. It was yards away

when we saw it again: a huddle of granite as near
as bereavement, like a small tomb, like fear

that had dragged us to face it from where
we were safe in the glen; unnerved and blinking here.

# THE PROPOSAL

*for Jo*

Beside the thin woodland stream
which runs full at this winter's end,
still this oasis of moss in the thorn
and blackberry bush and bracken,

the water running the same cold ribbon
through the flints' fingers (the infant ferns'
sea-horse shapes among the bracts of primrose
sheltered in the wood from the worst)

to the same dammed and secret pond
dinted by drowned trees and their roots
where, as planned, I stole on one knee
and made you laugh, thank God, before you'd say.

# AFTER THE FALL

1

Hospitals are 'hot and sad'
and make her feel ill, my daughter says.
I'd held my broken wrist like a broken wing,
walking the streets between the X-ray unit
and the *Maison de la Santé*

*Protestante*, in Nîmes: now, girded
by resin, in a sling, wincing until the panadol
slugs the pain (not the bone-end's grate so much
as a barbed asterisk, a drill's deep bit),
I discover how many are willing to say

they've been there, done it, showing me
the scars, the precise spot where it fissured, or the way
however hard they try they haven't got it back
quite as it was, twisting their hand like a doll's
or as if offering something of their own harm.

2

The dead have had their say
but the living hang around
for a little longer, meeting them

halfway, pretending
all they've done is high
drama and worth preserving:

my hand is a shoot off the root
of a plant in the birthday X-ray
and the broken wrist's that

dark parasite, introduced
by a lean on a ladder
too far, as if I was entranced

by something out of vision.
Cutting the cake, of late,
I've winced; but now the pain is true.


3

He cleaves the dirty mould
with a whining electric saw . . .

torture, or the idea of it – slipped
under, a metal bar is all that stands

between the psychotic circular blade
and what I can bear. Far

too casual, his expert's languor. Then,
like a well-split coconut, it's off!

A limp rag of a hand, the healed hinge
incapable even of acknowledgment . . .

thin, as if wasted, an empty haulm
that only needs the mind to fill it

with impulse, need, gesture –
the sugars flowing in like Fiorelli's plaster,

a split reed singing at the lips.

# MESSAGE IN A BOTTLE, 1968

The Congo River's slippage of brown lake,
so wide at times it might, for all one knows,
Niagara over the horizon's edge, unburdening
the weight of hippos (minnows in its wake)
and bobbing logs like twigs, swallowing pirogues
like seeds then thrashing to froth on rock
or shallowed suddenly by a sandbar,

tempted me to send it, probably, as far
as I could throw, like a stranded cartoon Crusoe
vying with the slim chances of root,
reef, net, surf-fleeced beaches tricked
out in whin or flesh, thalassic wrack
and thirty years or more of gathering storms
in which it still bounces like a periscope,

kept afloat by hope, not foundering, not flung
aside in dune-grass unopened by the lovers,
*To the person that finds me pleeease can you write*
not even swept beyond time's shimmering line
to my own hand, the tight cap sticky with Fanta still
and the spelling sound . . . as if regret might know itself
as something never found by another, only,

but visible in the ocean's vastness, over and over,
redeemed and floating, over and over in the swell.

# TROUBLES

I have the memory of the quay at Kinshasa,
yes, of leaning on the blebbed rail of the steamer
as it left behind the lined-up dads
dwindling into sheds and the blind
bush of a bend. Though what we fled had

spun lint turbans, blood-spotted,
around their heads and torn some collars
they grinned, nevertheless, sliding past us,
each side mimicking
the other's waves, as if glad to be gone.

A lot of dads, and behind them the invisible
mobs with chains, fabricated *pangas*,
the Congo's soft ovals of harm.
At any rate, what I remember
is not so clear that I cannot bear

the smothered feelings of loss, nor feel
the steamer's slow pulling away
in a tremble of throbs under my feet
some thirty-four years later, fearful still
(the airport closed, the pot-holed roads

mutinous with steam, a whole country's
steering gone) of growing up
and being left behind there, waving with
my sticking-plastered hand until
everything I love is lost beyond the bend.

# THE GARDEN OF THE
# FUGITIVES, POMPEII

*for P.Y.*

This is the gist of it: all our hurt, panic,
stuck in a row behind aquarium glass.

We sprint for our lives under the burning snow.
The man with the sack. The mother. The kid.

*Go*, we are told. They fled
to frayed faces where the teeth show through,

the mould come out at the elbows . . .
bone? I'd thought Fiorelli had filled

a void! But no, look, there is body
in them. And then

there is Pam, stretched
for a year already on a hospital bed,

able to move only her left eyelid.
Total paralysis. All the neurones down.

Just the lustre of eyes and the odd groan.
She wants to be dead but can't

quite be. So there
in her cage of bone it lies:

her garden, not quite fled.

# SACRIFICE

*The dead man who lay there was 2,000 years old . . .*
*consecrated for all time to Nerthus, goddess of fertility.*

P.V. Glob

*for Claus Bech*

I

Too close for comfort to the bog man
(Glob's Tollund, sleeping in peat,
for whom we'd come to Bjaeldskov Dal
camping wild among the ferny birch),

I rose in the night and grappled
out through darkness for a piss:
Danish cold, a kind of burr
of pine sweetness in the air

that needs the snow to smother it.
A walk alone over the fen
as dusk fell had already
throttled me with fear: all

at sea, divining my own death
in heartbeat twitches, lost
among briar and heather
where the sandy paths gave out

to the sombre ooze of pools . . . So,
in that same night's darkness,
the moonlight rent by leaves,
our two little domes of tents

scarcely suggested through the trees'
phantom stripes of bark,
I sensed as a medium might
in some Islington cabal

a second presence, no more than a hint,
watchful of me. And now my son,
more than two years later (and only
now), tells me how he lay

awake that night in terror, hearing
what he'd dared to peep on
pacing up and down, outside.
'A kind of man,' he says, 'all brown.'


2


Me? Or a divining of what
we went to only the following day

in the dim-lit room in Sikeborg?
Sleeved in temperature, asleep,

the body shrivelled to the leather
of its stitched hood, stubble

that gave that vexed, late-
night look under the calm

of someone who did not scream, it seems,
death succumbed to our gaze

on its lengthy pigtail of rope.
Earth's kindness is to hide us,

I suppose, but Tollund was pickled
in his own ghost, petrified

to an absorbed, ebony drape
of self, a landscape of ear

and shoulder, mudslipped waist,
those perfect striations of toes

squashed to geology: calmer
than the two just-drowned we found

that earlier summer (the end
being a state of mind), and ready

to rise from his grave portrait
to circle our guy ropes again,

I felt, that we might sense him
as more than in this room,

still-born . . . pacing up and down
with that slight pout of disdain,

yes, a pained frown on the brown
face, and moist as inside us.


3

I put his shrunken brain
to rest
in mine,

# FLEECE

*for M.K.*

'The dogs were really Elizabeth's,' he'd say,
'we had them all up North.' So I'd walk

the five of them on leads taut
as kitestrings in the freezing winds

of the winter downs, bare as steppe up there,
hoping to spot the shepherdess

(from the farm next door) bumping past in her jeep
or waving far off in a field

over a groundswell of wool.
Ours were rarer – mostly Jacobs

for their russet fleece, meant for the loom
gathering dust in the sitting room

from the day the Land Rover was hit by the wheel
that weirdly came from nowhere,

their last run down. 'Everything
on the skids since Elizabeth,' he'd say,

talking of her like a reign, not a wife –
a loss unredeemed by the sweetness of feed

clouding from the trough, or all his plans.
We'd mostly be having to mend, in fact.

Gates. The barn. Or the unstrung fence
that day of driving sleet in the lower field

by the stream – tamping around the posts
with the punners, stapling afresh . . .

The old, rusted snipes of wire
kept flaunting tufts of fleece

the year had purged of oil.
'The lovely stuff she'd spin,' he'd say

again and again, fingering the tobaccoey hairs
as though it was hers

he was seeing there, snagged
from her state of grace.

# THE JEWISH CEMETERY, CRACOW

*for my father-in-law*

Nettles crowd the avenues, giant ferns
jungle the corners under trees. The stones
rise above these like Mayan ruins, inclined

and cracked, their runes solemn under moss,
faint as tracks of birds that are all crows, here,
defying respect from the tree-tops

though scarcely heard above the hiss
and trickle of the heavy rain; too many leaves
and the headstones have turned into gulleys.

Neglect is its own care, but also means
someone's won, somewhere. We search
for hours in this green darkness,

tacking up and down, meeting each other
as if in sudden clearings. Carved names become
familiar; our trousers stick to our thighs.

The kids complain but not as much
as might have been deserved: the hunt's a game
and the place is a maze, for the tomb is not

where you remember in '35; the stretched
wake shuffling here, the sheer weight
of your grandfather's coffin on a teenage shoulder.

Ten or twelve more names chipped on since then
(you can't be sure) around '45 – but in one go,
without the heave of a body or the qualms

of mourners (who'd been mainly them).
History is a fraud whose lies are true
but this one stone of it we fail to find,

in the end, more bewildered than frantic.
No doubt we walked straight through it, as it were,
the rain hammering on our umbrellas – you

refusing to let it matter, of course, stiff-necked
as ever when it comes to remembering
such absurdity of loss. Nothing gained.

Later in the cathedral square we follow your finger
as it traces your walk from school, taking
your first vodka (in the very same café we sit in)

on a far-off afternoon, freed from the classroom.
The names on the stone we could not find
bob among your words – like ships, not flotsam:

you are their haven. They were here all along
where Cracow teems with the living
and your gestures show you as young among them again.

# NEOLITHIC

(West Kennet Long Barrow, c.3500 to 2500 BC)

1

We'd have done for them, anyway:
dope-heads, darkies, aboriginal scrum

of simpletons. Our home-grown gingery
version of the Apache, soon to become

gloom under stone, a litter of fags and condoms,
a forty-foot corridor of corbelled rock

rammed into Wiltshire and still, after all
these years, stiff under its jeans of downland.


2

For a rough ten hundred winters,
we know, they coughed around it, tending

their earthwork of slow-motion grief
in a running commentary of crows;

though silence comes off them like a smell.
Spina bifida twisted a few

of their spines, we can tell: a long insignia
of paralysis, a burr in the gods'

teasing of the wool. Of all their stories
(envy, murder, love, humiliation),

just one invented proper noun
and the stave-lines of absent adzes.


3

The mud's still shiny as gristle,
the trees blurred in the mist's daguerrotype

that shows me as a schoolboy, here,
alone, scraping, hoping for a find –

before the rich sods smashed my bicycle
and left it by the Chapel like a trophy.


4

We plough around their shadows so it shows,
scattered in the fields: East Kennet,

Liddington, Tidcombe Down . . . I'd wade
through grassland to get to them, or strike

off slowly through a seethe of barley
from Sugar Hill; dream I was theirs

but never, whistling inside, of death –
my elders, then, being almost everyone alive.


5

Now they're building them near Holsworthy
I read: not bell or bowl or disc, but thirty

low mounds like the Neolithic's: a grave
complex, a computer-catered knacker's yard,

a reek of gone-off eggs. Discreet, of course,
(the Danish for barrow means low),

the hundreds of thousands of cows compressed
in bin-liner smoulderings under floodlight,

it's patrolled day and night like an airbase;
*The Times* calls them (saving face),

'Pharaonic tombs . . . the future will wonder at,
as if some mysterious sacrifice has taken place.'

As though the gods won't know full well,
lowering their weight through the crows.


6

After I found my bike done in
(its delicate derailleurs contorted,

the broken chain coiled around the frame
in a double helix of greasy links,

the air fled from the tyres), I'd walk
to the barrows. It took more time,

though the time was mine. Anorak snapping
on the tombs like a cloak, I'd dream of kings,

the future sprawled like smoke or the corn
below. I did not know, I did not think

how history is mostly repair and revenge,
hurtling at you like the wind up there

on a winter morning: a dormitory
of bones and fear you thought far off,

dealt with, finished, long buried beneath.
But no, it's here, and you're the guest

and ghost, antlered and drawn and running.

# ODEMIRA

*Quem se lembra*
*da poesia*
*que nos contava em segredo?*

*for Manuel Branco*

We thought we'd meet a potter, met a poet
too; at the end of a long track
like a vein of thought running hidden off the road
he emerged in a white beard and slacks,

clay-thumbing spirit of the revolution,
*Com Homem Dentro*, the victory of the red carnation.
I told him in French how a toothless old crone
with her three-legged dog and wild gesticulations

had shown us where to go, like something out of myth.
'Cerberus,' he smiled, '*pas têtes, mais jambes.*'
The pottery shed had a cobwebbed look,
the kiln opening to a secret huddle he termed

his 'mistakes': flat open-throated flagons
for wine or flowers, the blue and cream
bubbled in places, completely 'missed'. I loved them –
the fish floating over trees, the boat flying as in dream –

and he sold them to me for a song.
We drank good beer on the wooden porch
of the long low adobe home (to celebrate, he said).
And talked. I felt I had stumbled on a mage.

He wondered why we'd come at all. I mentioned
the tourist-office pamphlet ('local crafts'),
asked him why he'd put no signs on the road
that faded to a lake under trees. He laughed.

'Signs bring trouble,' he said. 'I don't like signs.
If you want it enough, you arrive.'
He used to read to tens of thousands
at the height of it, he said, 'when I was still alive':

in Lisbon, in Paris, in Frankfurt. His best friend then
was now the prime minister. He remembered the rallies,
more fiery friends who'd made it. He had judged it wrong
and never compromised. We looked out on a valley

of cork trees, acacia, olives. Stillness.
His vegetable garden brimming with bees.
The dog of the German hippy down below
yapped at our legs. 'Our dream was this,'

he said. 'With decent schools and freedom. Not big roads.'
He sighed. 'All that's left for me is clay and rhyme.'
The dog yapped and nipped; he stood and yelled.
The German, pony-tailed, came up in his own slow time.

They conversed in English. The poet was angry.
'Europe,' he growled, afterwards. But we drank to hers
still, as if the porch was a plane and the whole bitch
stretched out eastwards under us, bombed by our verse.

# PETROGLYPHS

(Eastern Townships, Quebec)

*for Charles Lock*

I

Given nothing but an axe and a direction,
told to go where, in mosquito-clouded bush,

a rood of trees was theirs to make short work of,
they struck out west with their porcelain

and evening silks, their buckled-down bits
of Europe: just a razor's strop away

from the incurable Indian, that nakedness
the pocket Bibles fig-leafed. Now the land

is easy with its private rites, barbecues
snaking their smoke through the maples

on seamless lawns, the boats wobbling on the lake,
the chromium flash of wealth on the roads

between the stripling woods (the old ones felled).
They dropped in droves, the pioneers. Enough

to make one feel that cold and cholera
might have sufficed to leave the New World old,

standing here between these huddled graves
in a rough meadow where only the names are saved.

2

On Harry Jones's land near Vale Perkins
there's an 'Indian rock', I read,
where the Abenaki

scratched the story of a raid
on Fort Bridgeman
in 1755. No directions

or signs, so we gaze on the fenced hill's
tumble of boulders, knowing
how one among them speaks

of something so grave
it might have been the gods
that scraped, if we could find it;

but it would take us days.
Like one of those games
where the treasure's secreted,

or a family secret that shame
once concealed
from the gaze of strangers.

If only it was shame
that had! Instead,
this thistly, wired-off indifference.

This shrug of history.

3

My son and I, crashing through maple
on the final day, came across a boulder

on which signs were scratched all over;
faint white lines like signals from space.

No claw or tine could scrape such forms, we felt.
It was the old ones who were speaking

deep in the woods where no one walked
but a man and a boy, given sudden wings.

# RECENT SUMMERS

This imminence . . . an English distillation
of lowering hedges, a hammer-weight of heat

on the accomplishing ferns: everything tending
to cataclysm, fiddling while even dawn burns.

We wait: things might get worse (the hearse
ticking by the cemetery gate). The silence of the birds

we don't look up to, now we're up to things.
The calm freight of clouds too late to count.

# FRED'S TREASURE

'Still gas,' he chuckled, back in '76,
strengthening the wall-lamps' whiteness. 'I'm the last

darn house in Chesham, now.' The rooms were a wade
of cardboard boxes – from which he'd pick, wrapped

in sheaths of the *Bucks Examiner*, his collection's gems.
Mainly flints. The coulter's clang had betrayed them

to him, trawling the plough-lines in its wake;
tell-tale swells and trims, purposeful, flaked –

nothing chance did: all enacted, shaped.
God knows why he'd begun, as a kid, to the creak

and cluck of a horse-team, in a blizzard of gulls,
but his passion'd found itself in furrows

up Buckland Common, or down near Chartridge,
over Botley way or in the thick

chalk of Cholesbury where the hill-fort is.
He let me palm a bulk of Clactonian axe,

smoothed by bone to a meat-red shine, that the BM
craved to have. 'Oh no, it stays, I said.'

I'd brought him mine to check, in a Co-op bag:
a pyx of flints from walks and a curve of bone,

pick-like, he might have laughed at. Well, you could
have drystone-walled a field with what he'd found:

chopper, spear-tip, scraper, core; axe-heads,
chisels of bone, a jaw . . . the lofty drudge

of a lifetime, that – that only just fought shy
of sadness, for all his love had knapped

it into jewels. Dulled, I suppose, the moment
he was gone (as with all our things)

to a frass of boxes full of pointless rocks
in a gassy semi, near the water-cress beds.

# FLESH AND BLOOD

*Feel my hands*, you'd say: *like ice!* –
hugging the radiator in the warm room;

certainly a little chill, the touch
of your elderly skin. Proof of age,

by which, of course, you were still amazed –
as I am now at how the speech from *Hamlet*

on the BBC (reissued) tape
revives that touch, as real

as the press of a piano's key: the dead
don't quite leave off for good. *I could*

*a tale unfold whose lightest word*
*would harrow up thy soul, freeze*

*thy young blood* – your voice
still under it, bewitching my childhood

between the easy chairs in Chesham,
*Hamlet* dawning as a domestic god . . .

Your own blood, old, slowed right down
until sherry went straight to your head

and our lunches would end in the ambulance,
your gashed leg oozing a syrup

that was almost cold, that scarcely ran
from the too-soft skin that time

it hung like a stocking. Hell
was living too long, you said –

surviving a husband you'd miss each day
by forty years, London a prison

of trip-wire pavements and dextrous shoves
and the eternal flight of stairs to your nutshell room.

# THE CHANCES ARE

(Campo Santo, Pisa)

Swifts squeal where the firebomb fell –
bouncing off the cloisters' roof

and sparing, from a wealth
of *quattrocento* frescoes

only one, like a kind of proof: *The Triumph
of Hell*. The rest worn down to brick

in an hour or two. As, quite suddenly,
at a certain age (say, forty-five),

what you could have done but did not try
(the career on the stage, the moving

to Amsterdam) arrives from the sky
and rubs its ebullient, painstaking flame

on your fixed tempera, scene after scene:
the wasted opportunities, the best of a life.

Though the chances are those charred walls
would've shuttled into place the same.

# YOUR NAME IN FULL

The Old Norse still clinging there
like something a frog might do

in a Danish bog
or the sound I'd make

on that temple slughorn my father bought
in Katmandu in '58

or what those huge coiling snakes of bronze
older than Vikings, thunder-booms

slumbering behind glass in Copenhagen's National Museum
might wake to

at the sour breath of Ragnaroth:
*porp.*

The other uniquely
mine, caudled in affection,

tag of love so familiar
it was cleanly, clearly me

until the Bible lesson
in '63 –

Genesis, the Garden of Eden.
Myself surging from the words

and the class erupting in squeals
as I walked in the cool of day with Eve

between the trees,
Miss Scott smiling shyly as she read,

relentless, to the bell –
then, in the playground,

a scrimmage as the fingers
tickled, let rip,

clambering up the ladder of my ribs
and down again

searching for the missing rung
in all seriousness,

fervent as punishment
or a girl's kiss.

And in the middle, yes,
the scrupulous secret,

shaming for no real reason;
an old family surname

rattling on through generations . . .
a piece of forgotten root, a filler

shared with my father
that makes a disastrous acronym of name –

A.N.T. An
ugly shadow, a haunting

like the hand-me-down Roman nose
or the strain of something botched

or the old, forgotten loyalties
of clan, of kin: something

only vaguely my own,
product of duty or sheer whim,

uncalled for until
some real shame rings it

out at last in leaden strokes –
hammered to the open, collared, caught:

your name in full
like the spy within

who knows much more than he ought
and might just tell

but I'm not telling you.
(So just as well

the front-page court report
in the *Marlborough Advertiser*

back in '82
had 'Adam Naylor Thrope',

and no one knew.)

# THE CAUSEWAY

It was only a rowing-boat, back in those days;
one-man crew, potato-sacks and gossip,

too small for a car. So the tiny island bred
its own species: unlicensed, dented, mirrorless,

treads as if sea-smoothed, the milometer
seized from lack of use, like a swift's legs –

there was nowhere to go but round,
quicker to walk it from here to there.

Yet their elders were everywhere, abandoned
where they'd died whining or kept

for the hens; dashboards losing their toggles
and wires, mudguards curved in the rust

of autumn ferns . . . while the whole place,
it seemed, champed to be further off

from the other isles, like abandoned
St Kilda with its birds. And now? The causeway

cuts the choppy water in a marriage-
knot: no longer the longing of sea miles

but a few hundred yards on sound tyres.

# PRINTS

The dollardom shore of big Lake Michigan
finds him doing what he did as a boy

by real seas, running alongside them:
the land's hem stitched, he'd look

back upon a long beach emptied
by twilight (his spoor blurred as if already

old), and turn it to Avalon, or Crusoe's island.
Even on the edge of Central Africa

he had to change into somewhere else
what they would always be alone with

after the bush-drive; imagining this
not ever seen, not watched, kept

locked from eyes like a schoolgirl's journal –
older than lungs, earlier even than gill slits

or the hair-like cilia of bivalves, the sea-edge
stroking backwards through deep time

and the blasts of geology, silvering his prints
from laval sand with the stands of palm-trees

cupped from sight by his hand . . . then find,
on the slow walk back, an impress or two

the sweeps of foam had missed: fossils
of some unknown future, or ears listening

through billions of years of hiss for the delicate cry.

# LAGO NERO

Solitary, a steep two-hour walk
up the snow-limed, winding track
to the lone chapel with its locked

clutter of pews in the gloom,
its painted Mary emerging
far, one felt, from her home:

a rumour of someone known.
Old notices, as in some English porch.
A worn-out cross in the stone.

I spot a scintillant of jet
in the sheer sky above the soft
white outcrops of mountain, the black

lake disguised as a deer-tracked
flatness under a glare of snow,
the jet's suggestion of a roar erupting

like an afterthought, the truth
arrived at! I have, instead, a sudden
hunch – the faintest scar of worry, really –

that even heights like these are the hour's
stooge: the grandest mountains give
in time. And I see it like a diagram,

almost educational – moraine,
landslip, friction, wind: the solid
gleam of the perpetual as sheer idea

and thought its isopleth, that links
like point with like point
until we become what we meant

to be all along, but did not dare.

# NERVE

*in memory of Sébastien Houix*

I

'I'm immensely privileged,' you say, paralysed
from the neck down and hardly able to speak.

Your hands rise to the mouse in mine, are left
there; their twitch shifts the arrow round

the on-screen keyboard. Your fingers feel like snow
crust, but the words you coax from them

are warmed with care, each laid down like leaves
of gold by time (a day to phrase a thought) –

and pain, no doubt. Your cup of tea with its straw
turns cold, resting on its book. The weeks

are up and down, but you're aware in writing
(I quote from the poem) of your steady aim: 'to stay

alive until the cows come home'. A dream, we know:
the doctors said you wouldn't see the summer

I'm looking out for on the breeze like a sign:
the fragrance of thyme against the burning odds.


2

The heat's full on, the cicadas brimming,
a slow slap of coldness in the stone *bassin*.

My brilliant student, ten years on from London you're lying
in the shade of your Aleppo pine, being read to again.

You're always smiling. Now it's the turn of the breath
to come with an effort. Next week they'll bring

a machine with its mask's relief. 'It's very tiring
to breathe,' you tell me in gasps, 'but I think

it's the heat.' Everything else – the nerve-logged
muscle, loss of weight, the way the head now lolls

too heavy for you – you have taken on board; but you
refuse this slack from the lungs. So the cool of autumn's

looked forward to: Brittany, a trip to the sea.
'To watch the storms,' you explain. A simple

phrase that leaves you beached, choking. Just
turned thirty, scalloped to the bone, you're fighting

for the right to return to your element: air,
love, movement. I see you there in the teeth

of some Atlantic gale, spindrift flying by your chair,
grinning on a cliff-top. Outfacing the bare

facts, the unjust laws that sink a survivor.
Your wit, for instance, still makes me laugh,

each word retrieved from some deep mine
of life. If wit alone was sufficient to stall

whatever's pinned you here, choking in its creep,
you'd pick up your chair and walk, Seb,

running your voice through the resinous
*sotto voce* of the pines and the river, then diving there.


3

I'm reading you Shelley. A tiny fly
flickers on your face. I brush it off.

It returns through the verse, crawls over your forehead
undisturbed, as if you're dead; even in sleep

your hand can't lift to scratch, or brush away –
though you tell me you dream of it, and of moving

like the young man you are through bars and streets.


4

You'd shape the garden from your seat,
the bamboo sheared halfway, the flowers

scattered with precise care
along the paths your electric chair

bumped on, the old pond scoured
and put to fish, each order gasped

in Spanish. You called yourself
'Lord', with that mischievous grin,

reckoning you had 'all the power
of a petty despot' (unable to lift a finger

at whim – or anything). Most times you were
stilled, contemplating, so quiet

it was hard to make you out
under the *chênes verts.* 'I'm the luckiest

man alive,' you'd claim, when you could still
speak; 'I can watch the light, actually

watch it move through an entire day.
You see? Watch how the sun creeps leaf to leaf,

the shadows, the birds, the sounds. I feel
at one with everything,' you'd add, in hoarse

gasps, dappled there in the trees and become
your own sundial, stilled, slowing things

down until they might go back as they were.


5


Soon you spoke only through the letters
clustered in groups on the square of perspex

I'd nestle on my lap, peering over it
as you moved my finger with your eyes' roll,

patient as dry-point: your four languages
stroked out of it, the mother-tongue French

reserved for your mother – commanding her
like an infant's tell-tale cries, again. There was

a magic, though, in that slowed-down spell:
*PERT . . . IN . . . what? IN . . . what? IN . . . ENTL?*

Ah! *LY! PERTINENTLY SAID,* you'd said,
and were saying it now with that ventriloquist's grin

that brooked no short-cuts, not even *TEA?* – as if
the grammar's knitting of a full-blown phrase

(*HOW ABOUT A CUP OF TEA*
or, *WHOS TO SAY IT WOULD HAVE MADE*

*MUCH DIFFERENCE I AM HAPPY NOW*)
was itself a shield, see-through but unshatterable . . .

along with the jokes, of course: as when those two distant
relatives from Aix, stooped over you, were shouting

questions for the deaf, the slow ('*Et comment vas-tu?*
*Tu as tous qu'il te faut?*), and my finger's

acknowledgment built from your eyes
*THEYRE GHASTLY,* in English disguise.


6


The day you had to go to the hospital
for the stomach tube, you were asked

if you wanted to take anything
and you said, letter by letter on the perspex

page (I translate), *MY TENNIS RACQUET*. And then,
signalling something more to be added

through the laughter of those who could move
and speak and breathe without pain,

you had them pluck from the strings of letters
*DO YOU RECKON THEY HAVE ANY BALLS*

*AT THE HOSPITAL*. Two days later you were dead.
Your last words to the nurse? *BON COURAGE*.

# MARKET DAY

I always stop before the fossil stall
when the market comes round to summer
like a fleet of sampans and billows
with striped awnings that shade

gewgaws, baubles, things only
the slow magpie tourists need –
curios for the bored who believe
it is like this here all the time.

*And what do I know? Nothing.*
I think this again, on pause
before the simple trestle
of the fossil stall. There must

somewhere be abundance of them
for they are the same each time,
authenticated in a string of zeroes,
a hand-written *Cambrien* or *Carbonifère* –

even the dinky, idling teeth
deleted from early sharks, or the gnat
snagged in boiled-sweet amber
I roll in my palm. A glimpse

of coincident eternity, chance
rendering a flicker immortal, less
likely even than some still-room full
of these whiffs of olives and wine,

our prattling voices over the church bell,
the tremble of the melon man's
hands weighing, the weight of potatoes
in the basket, the sheepfold

shiftings of the crowd, or the sourness
of the mayor (with his clutch of gourds
and honey-pots) who hates me;
all these frailer than a whale's ear-bone

or this spiral galaxy of ammonite
in its jet-black slate . . . Far frailer,
in fact: for these are written for good
in stone, these trails of tails and burrowings

or the pricier ancient fish
dimly X-rayed on plates of sand
where they sank to, drowned, flat as plaice
and boned from oblivion to be a souvenir

sheer chance rescued from time as we
will not be, now, crowding here
between the summery stalls and smiles
and the sour hatred of the mayor.

# MIGRAINE

Inadequacy: caries of the brain,
sugared by loneliness. Roots so deep

it conjures an iron crown
bolted to the bone, but growing,

growing. Migraine's grey house.
The brilliance of snow on fake trees

and the flash of jingles.
And what if this was said to be enough

for a whole lifetime?
The skull a sarsen of its own pain

like the girl's skidded into by the car
who said, on *France Inter*,

that every second now
was *une vraie galère* for good,

and that she couldn't forgive.
And what if she could?

Would the stone be lifted by a flight of angels?
Would the undulations flatten to a calm?

2

The pain's organised, like crime:
the feel it has of cool forests

falling and falling inside me –
my head a cartoon Earth, perhaps,

with vinegar and brown-paper
poultice, the sun beating down

on the clear-cut forests, my eyes'
two washed-up fish that are the bad sign.

# SNOWED UP

*for Kim*

Roads erased, but the milk warm
from the one farm a way was dug to,

the ladle tinkling on the churn we queued for
like Alpine herds. 'The Lapps

lined their boots with sennegrass,'
someone chuckled, stamping his.

Stranded, becalmed in a glacier's air,
news from nowhere, all tidings gone,

the TVs flickering to candlelight alone.
Tsunamis of drifts, with shrieks going down;

the pond and green become the same swell.
Seraphs of flint-glass, three days old,

their carrot noses pockmarked by the birds
and starlight glittering on the dared-on downs.

The fresh grew stained, and crunched
like apples. Shovels ringing instead of phones.

And the butcher was down to brains,
trotters, eyeballs ('which I recommend'),

when, in the drift-bound bus stop, you brushed
its times into view like a buried capsule

and sat there waiting for the Swindon one,
determined to leave, late already.

And patient for the purr of an engine
as you were, gratefully mistaken,

you might have sat it out till nightfall
clutching your backpack, ready with the change,

but for the unnerving fathoms of the cold
and the looks, amazed, from those who saw.

# PRODUCTIVITY

*after George Ewart Evans*

To bring the bloom onto the horses' coats
at dawn, each day, before the ploughing . . .
tansy leaves rubbed between the hands
and sprinkled in the bait; or sweet
saffron, baked to dry
and fed in the same way – though not too much
or the sweat would bring the powder out
and the horse would smell of saffron.

Or cut-up bryony root, fed
into the chaff; you'd come across it
ditching, and grate it on the wife's
nutmeg grater: it cleaned the skin wonderfully, men
and beasts. Or a wet of piss on the chaff
would make the coat shine.
Or black antimony to get that bloom,
or rubbing him down lightly with a rag

dipped in paraffin – that also
kept the flies off and held him steadiest in the show-ring.
Or a few leaves off the box hedge
dried and fed in a powder in the chaff
kept the sweat down that spoiled the shine.
And gentian or felwort to keep his appetite,
bring him back to the rack
and manger. Mangels from the bullocks' barn

ground up, that toned them up, too,
April time, just after coming out of the clamp.
And into the open field
after two hours' grooming, turning out to plough
at 6.30 a.m. with a shining team
for the strong loam and leaving the furrows
without a wrinkle to mar the whole length of it . . .
that kept you on your toes, that did,

they did, did the horses.

# PLAY IT AT FORTY-FIVE

Too like a Dutch town, my mind:
well-behaved, no sudden ululations

of grief or despair, no wild
shaman dances of admiration

for the attendant gods; more
the discreet frown that hinges on propriety,

my bill of care the slight pucker
of indigestion, of life going down

too easily, too fast. I am rarely
startled, these days, and my dreams

are an iconography of trains
I'm always running for but seldom miss

though they never arrive where I think
they might, amid the dated hiss

of everything I ought to have done
beyond the sign of caution, slowing down.

# GHOSTS IN THE BATHS OF CARACALLA

The gloom beyond the roadside planes expands
to a Chicago skyline of shattered brick,
a labyrinth of half-domed halls that sounds
with the squeals of swifts, like children, like a trick

of light on polished, fish-drawn tiles; we're almost
persuaded. We wade through clumps of grass instead,
stand on the marble lips of a dried-up past
and try to find what the guidebook said

about *tepidarium*, noting the pipes and drains.
Steam-bath vapours, hazed windowlights,
the fear of verrucas and showing the stains
on your underpants, changing; the boards' heights

higher than your vanity; the sting of bleach
gathering like crumbs under the eyelids. The girl
who drowned on Opening Day in Amersham, unable to reach
air through the ganglion legs and turning to pearl,

lying unseen all day at twelve foot six while
life thrashed above her in its usual style,
lies here, too: Roman, now, and dignified
by all these who've enjoyed themselves and died.

# BLUEBERRY PICKING
## IN MICHIGAN

*for Lucy and Hugo Wistreich*

Along with the orchards' Main Street-straight straight rows
and the Pick-Your-Own bunch of families' cries

('Where are you, honey . . .?' 'I'm here, right here!')
through the stripes and shots of sunlight between the leaves

the farm's to be sold, we're told. 'Lucy, I'm beat.
It's sixteen hours a day and I'm gettin' old.'

The final harvest and it's hard to believe
when all it takes is a twist and a squeeze

for each fat pap to be tumbled to fruit
that peppers neck-slung panniers or spills to be juiced

on the ground: how crazy to think this can all be razed
where abundance itself's a kind of law, a right!

Our baskets are heavy, the day too warm. My son's
showing me how the blue rubs off to a shine as black

as a mouse's eyeball (though black is really blue, deep down) . . .
Sorcerer-lipped, indigo-woaded, we grin like clowns

as the farmer ribs us on our return: the original
sin in the garden, and how we'd 'better git up

on the scales, too, you guys, judgin' by your faces!'
The Last Day beckons in the sign erected there already

on the road: *Prime Land for Real Estate* with so
many acres. Orchards just don't pay, you say, these days –

'even in Michigan, Garden of the World': the coming season's
mashed-up soil ruled off to plots, zoned for the diggers.

It'll ripen to something though, I suppose: lawns in the blueberry
light of dawn; glistening sidewalks under snow; seep

of fries and hysteria of TVs ('While they're
too nice with curd,' the farmer's saying), or a dim phone

continuing on through the middle of an afternoon.

# CORDIAL

## (Corrèze)

The stuffed fox's cobweb runs from its nose
to the rusted tins of sugar on the chimneypiece;

the black pot's slung above the smouldering log
and pulses steam. The walls have been smoked out of whiteness

to the rusty brown of a windfall, almost golden;
hold dated calendars and beehived nudes

pinned and curling like bills in Dutch still-lives.
He was feeding the pigs outside, the bent old man;

now we are with him among the dark benches,
the one big table hidden under a welter of papers.

The sign may be broken but he's hung on here for fifty years,
'*toujours ouvert*'. We order some *sirop* for the kids.

Glugged out of a dusty, retro-labelled bottle
swirling with sediment, it leaves a corona

where the level's stayed put too long, it seems;
smells vaguely methyl, though it's *grenadine*.

He thins it down tumbler by tumbler under
the doddery tap. 'There's something wrong,' Josh hisses,

'taste it!' Like a forest floor it's fermented
into strength, mellow as island malt

from not being asked for for God knows
how many years. He's telling us of his stretch,

'during a man's best time', as a prisoner of war –
come back too old for '*les filles*', he stayed

celibate, uncourted; the unstirred spirit steeped
only in its own hour, here between the trees.

We walk back home in awe, unsteadied by a
child's drink: that someone can just live

there where it is good, accreting the years like leaf
fall, altering nothing, strikes me as rare and fine –

if only that strength could be foreseen, like wine.

# EXILE

England, royal-revelation-awash,
(muck's sluice-tide) barely holds her head

above the waters of her own front page,
the rustling, thrown-away woods of her mind.

Murrain. War. Fame. What was it Eliot
said? Those who sharpen the tooth of the dog . . .

One day you will show me a perfect creature
of small cornfields and vales, sunlight

on spires, towns cosy behind their walls
and love at the sharp end of age.

# TRACKS

Up in the Alps
on a fair day of snow-sheets
we tracked a rabbit

to a sudden hiatus
of blood and fur.
*Fox*, I said – not knowing

any better, but excited
by something vinous and heady
to show the kids:

as if life doesn't
always come
spotting the bland snow

with its bright
abruptness – or doesn't
so clearly now,

pound-foolish
with beast, bird and forest,
drawing the curtain

like a white drift
over the way (mistaken
for the hard path underfoot)

to the blizzard's cliff.

# SCRATCHINGS

*Jour enselevi que la poésie dégage comme la bêche la source*
                                                    Yves Bonnefoy

I

If America, her spirit of anywhere lives
it is here, on Rockford's frayed edge

of diners, malls, neon, cross-stitch freeways.
Rained on in storm and exhaling the burnt offering

of summering cement, tarmac, the lawn surround
of a Burger King on its midnight strand of parking.

The woman, skin-ruffed, grimly at the counter
with headphones, lipmike, lonely in the fall

of frosty light, takes our orders and calls.
Lonely Hopperish all-night brightness,

lonely buzz of the kitchens' electrics like anxiety.
Madness. Madness in the absence of prairie, here –

something deadly numbed not there that should be.
Is this precisely where (this spot) the Sioux,

for instance, spied their non-gods
in loneliness of fasting, creatures of earth and air,

the solemn hide-flap of the tipi opening
to a universe speeding from the eyes like horses

to no known end but the end of breathing?

2

Gods? Have done with them.
Gods obscure the woods, the stones, the moon,
on a hanging edge the beech golden that combs down to the
    coomb
or the fox fleeting narrowly beneath it that one morning.

The sparrow-hawk spotted by us tree-nursery workers
knelt to the inching oaks, their leaves frost-dotted,
dawn then like a polished stone, flint
to fire all along, goaded us to pray but we didn't.

Or the Essex marshes by the Sainsbury depot
from the train like something consoling seen, waving
rushes and the blades of floods over acres.
Have done with them all in majesty of sea water, woods.


3

Shuttered laundrette in a morning haze,
damp's vaseline and the smell of feet
in the shop where the news is baled
on the floor to trip me up, the shuffle

of the old black guy at the corner with his Asda bags:
all this unchanging, as if in Latin, a tower-block
merely the interruption of the laconic barbarian,
Bedlam still there where it stood, bottom of Eastcheap,

my suitcase careering on its wheels
behind me, running, late (bomb scare on the Tube),
stopping this guy – an Australian – to check,
who tells me with great concern

not to go further than Waitrose, mate.
Everyone whelmed by what's under, not above, old
places for burial whose skeletons resemble the insane
screaming through portholes, silenced, in pain going down.

In the train's funnelling fury I find
a fresh language, as London once after fire did,
ransacked, gutted: *What was doing it was that open
sea-chest.* And the speaker serious in a grey suit.


4


The school's gull-cries even from the stumbling path
down to where my daughter's already alight with release,
coming home. My own home-comings in Chesham,
long levelled light of evening, the bus windows misting

so blankly one day I missed the stop and went right on
to where I didn't know, no longer crack-hopping on familiar ways
but abandoned to my own whereabouts in a large road; and
     remained
but to walk, ask, vague directions right to my mother's alarm that
     lateness

made dream of things no child should know, mist-bound and
     blissful.


5


So close to madness the scooter accelerated of its own accord,
braked at the roundabouts and junctions, *took* me to my place.

So mad the electric heater beamed *itself* to life, clicked off
while you were thinking of me. Aglow enough with longing.

So mad I might be, oblivion's second chance, the hedgerow
becoming a maze, feeding off wood sorrel and lapping at where

the brambles touch me. So mad I might be, in the dim
twilight of woods, your deadleaf-coloured stroke of fortune

falling into sunlight or far-off clash of trolleys like wind-stroked
    wheat
where once wheat was – and before that the madness of pure trees.


6


Dante your uncle, kind, who looked into the snake eyes
of the SS guard in Warsaw, kin to oblivion, sudden; chance luck;
lost all his family who didn't mind the omens deep in the spine,

who survived on berries in Polish woods, daring himself down for
    bread,
has died, is burned to ashes and his ashes spread in Kenwood
    under a particular tree
by the gravel walk he loved and will always remember,

his pots the colour of pools and trees and moments one
    remembers
as moments, his swift brush-strokes strokes of memory one waits
    for
for hours, sometimes: branch, blossom, bird, berry.
    Unfortunately born,

to arrive at the moment when promise was burned, exile,
family not buried, smoke above the ghetto, the Ukrainian colonel
head-tapping casually the queue, every other man, to the firing
    squad

(closest friend so tapped in front of him), Dante survived
to fire in ash his bowls that require (he said) a whole wall of white
emptiness behind, limned by the ash-breath of art.


7

Lead mines such as they were dug by Romans
on moors where the Thorpes had land, mute tussocks
coming to no more than a few acres 'somewhere up there' –
my father waving his hand in the car as we passed

and me yearning, on grassed slopes mottled by cow's dung gazing
and on the buckled barbed wire about the lead mines
'fallen into disrepair', deep and dangerous, harbouring
skulls of those who called for a while, and no one to hear them.


8

Bramble-hid, the little fall of stream that no one sees,
night-noise of tiny Niagara roar under the clear stars

and smell of water. I once made love under a tree
with a clear view over pasture heights

and was barely screened, wincing at roots
and acorns, the clue of dead leaves on the duffel

brushed before home. The origin of writing is indents
in bare skin, verse of water under the covers hidden,

love-cry under the sky's openness in March's Berkshire cold,
lying on uncomfortable roots and sheep-dung, exposed to one's
 land.


9

I knew waiting for school's boarding by the bingo hall in Watford
the coach would come, the inevitability of deathly things,

sad things, the sadness in me always like a thorn, coach-sick –
then staring at my reflection in the coach's glass

as it trembled up the broad road past homes and windows
to the black Wiltshire spaces, downs, like space itself

a vacuum into which I am thrown, the pure unknown,
reluctant, sickly with fear, bullies' thrones on knees before,

sick for home or for my own career, not bred for this,
England-outsider, not quite stranger but not friend either, nor foe.


10

Vapour hazing the valley, mournful all morning, though
at two in the afternoon the sun breaks through

and curtains the view in shafts below dark cloud,
hill after hill descending to the plain in blues and greys,

watercolour country today, but oil usually,
sharp, though all grey shades say painters when the sun's not

glittering on the leaves of ilex, every
hill draped with ilex as downlands with grass,

the breaks of vines autumnal in red and orange,
the impossible-to-capture groves of olives

puffed like smoke, and the sharp little flames of poplars.
Countless times I've been up here behind

our house, yet never described it; Blanche's castle
sitting on its saddle over haze like a conning tower

and sprawled around it the sea-green pines and ilex,
the odd half-buried roof of a farmhouse down to the village

and way out sometimes the line of silvering sea when the light
   is clean
and the sharp little teeth of the Alps on their mimicking cloud.


II

Not surer than this as stone is, slabs of it,
sunlit in Nîmes where a Roman company

slumped to from Egypt conquerings, notable massacres –
war-excused as always have been, bombs and civilians

marrying in pain's ensign of smoke, ghastly
wet wounds glimpsed then talk only of equipment,

Rome's hardware the same though not these planes,
not the finesse screwed up to *such* destruction, quarry

a pinpoint number, heartbeat turned to vague green star
and out of it all Nîmes' beauty coming like a captured woman

freed on the plain, not crocodile at all on its lead
but a woman, graceful, in ivory of old stone

and olivey skins, Spanish-Arab, French like an afterthought,
the water whelming there in the Jardins de la Fontaine

that Henry James thought perfect in its way,
the mysterious source of water poured like a blessing,

oasis in the dry plain of suddenly-pointless mammoth aqueduct
as some time we shall have no use for anything essential now.

# HONESTY

*Lunaria rediviva*

There is honesty everywhere, we see,
on our long road back from Germany
this Easter of war; sprawled on verges
and road-banks, scattering its lilac,

honesty was even in that grey village
with its two *routiers* and the alcoholic chef
(thundered through by lorries escaping the tolls),
where we searched for a bed. It's rained all day,

and honesty thrives on the wet slopes
and the earth-spills near those broken sheds
of some long-abandoned enterprise
or in the slim gleam of the beechwood.

Honesty, though wild, is rare in the wild
yet here it seems to outdo the rest,
the ramsons and knapweed and stitchwort.
A few days back in Germany we saw it

garden-tamed, filling a bed
in a village encircled by the Teutoburg forest
where Arminius fell upon the legions of Rome,
whooping and wailing and wheeling

into them until they were as gone
as extinct species, felled like trees
under the darker trees, armour
thumping on the soft pine-mould

through the screams and moans, the snortings
of gored horses. The honesty
was serried into a square between
a pink rose-bush and the mown lawn

where plastic toys were liberally
scattered; it was almost a statement,
the toys and the honesty, though the villa
itself was as trim as could be. I wondered, then,

whether honesty's look – gawky stems
where petals attempt some point and class
against rough-toothed, careless leaves –
is a fall from cultivated grace

or one step up from a former state:
is ascent or decline . . . At any rate, I allow it
to flower where it will in my own
garden; a wind's cast off

from last year's blooms, the few always
appear in a new position, half
a surprise, half an expectation – their flat
seed-pods gathered to be dried, silvery

as coins once the film's peeled
then tarnished by months of household dust
to something awkward caught on sleeves . . .
as if honesty in all its states is made

to be a not-quite thing, neither one
nor the other, neither here nor there;
a half-cock, an in-between, too common,
too rare. I would have it sown

in thick clouds everywhere, that honesty
might rise, unexpected, from rifts and cracks
in drifts of lilac, like thunder, like seas,
happy with its wildness and not waiting on us

to judge or decide, who know only lies.